Everything I Know *I Learned from* My Grandpa

Silver-Haired Wisdom *for the* Young *at* Heart

Paintings by
Jack Sorenson

HARVEST HOUSE PUBLISHERS

EUGENE, OREGON

EVERYTHING I KNOW I LEARNED FROM MY GRANDPA

Text copyright © 2006 by Harvest House Publishers
Eugene, Oregon 97402

ISBN-13: 978-0-7369-1629-5
ISBN-10: 0-7369-1629-6

Artwork © Jack Sorenson Fine Art, Inc. and may not be reproduced without permission. For more
information reagrding artwork featured in this book, please contact:

Rich Wiseman, LLC
Fine Art and Gift Licensing
7 Avenida Vista Grande #250
Santa Fe, NM 87508
(505) 466-1927

Text by Hope Lyda

Design and production by Koechel Peterson & Associates, Inc., Minneapolis, Minnesota

Printed in China

06 07 08 09 10 11 12 13 14 / IM / 10 9 8 7 6 5 4 3 2 1

In memory of
Grandpa Dick VanderMeulen

Grandparents are similar
to a piece of string—
handy to have around
and easily wrapped
around the fingers of
their grandchildren.

—AUTHOR UNKNOWN

Grandparents, like heroes, are as necessary
to a child's growth as vitamins.
—JOYCE ALLSTON

Why We *Love* Our Grandpas

Grandfathers first appear in our lives as mysterious extensions of our parents. Tall. Strong. Short. Intellectual. Funny. Serious. Tough. Gentle. However they first impress us, there is something immediately special about these men who hand us chocolates wrapped in cellophane, who laugh generously at our clumsy jokes, or who point our wide eyes toward a shooting star.

Smelling of aftershave and mints, grandpas patiently listen to us share the joys of our childhood. We eagerly tell them about our discoveries and our achievements. And we gladly climb up beside them in a big, worn chair to hear tales of their lives and to share a bit of our own. Grandpas lead our first classroom sessions on the front porch and at the old kitchen table as talks about weather, the reason for cocoons, and why grass is green stretch spring days into summer nights.

When we are little and long to be heard, grandpas kneel down and take interest in the bug on a limb or the scrape on our elbow. The security and pleasure of being understood and cherished helps us grow into confident teens, strong adults, and more attentive friends, parents, and even grandparents.

The image of our grandfathers remains with us as the years go by. Memories haloed in golden hues might be embellished or rewritten by our mythical sense of these men, but the memories are always real—for they help shape our understanding of love, courage, kindness, and family. They give us what we need for our own journey.

Grandchildren are the dots that connect the lines from generation to generation.
—Lois Wyse

We All Belong

In the heat of summer, my sister and I spent many hours riding in the backseat of a blue Chevy Impala, entertaining ourselves with a stash of Weekly Reader books and imaginative performances, using our feet as puppets on the back window stage. These trips from Iowa to Oregon to see my grandparents were big adventures compared to our usual summer activities: countless games of kick the can and biking up and down the cul-de-sac with playing cards clothespinned to the spokes. And while we could have been upset to have our neighborhood time interrupted by a cross-country trip, we enjoyed the journey and anticipated the loving welcome we would receive in Oregon.

*   *   *   *   *   *

Once we arrive and get our share of hugs, we rush upstairs to scout out our rooms and take a tour of the large, white house we know so well from previous visits. This room used to be Mom's. That room used to be Aunt Carol's. The closets are big enough to build forts in—we don't, but we love that we could. Steep stairs lead down to the cool basement where Grandpa's punching bag and old-fashioned phone both require a stepping stool to reach. The camper in the driveway is open for us to pretend we are waitresses in a café until we are called inside to a real dinner.

On our way to the large dining room table, we stop at the kitchen cupboard. Standing on tippy-toe we scan the rows looking for the drinking glass with our name etched via a label maker. We reach for it, and hold it as evidence that we are part of this family, this household, and this home.

As a child, I never felt like an intruder in my grandparents' home. And my grandfather's strong personality never overwhelmed our tentative, budding ones. He treated us like thinking individuals and never spoke down to us. He even included us in a game of Yahtzee or dominoes should we accept the challenge.

Today, most of us represented by the label names in my Grandparent's cupboard have permanently claimed our glass. And each time we open up the cupboard in our own kitchens and see our name in white against the colored label, we welcome back the memories of those summers with Grandpa and the sense of belonging.

*Nobody can do for little children
what grandparents do.
Grandparents sort of sprinkle
stardust over the lives
of little children.*
—ALEX HALEY

7

Perfect love sometimes does not come
until the first grandchild.
—Welsh Proverb

We Were *Never* Visitors

I became a grandpa for the first time 18 months ago to a wonderful grandson named Isaac. Like a lot of grandpas, I'm a long-distance grandparent. In a way, the miles between Isaac and me have heightened the joy and appreciation for the times I have with him. I have a strong desire to know Isaac and be known by him as his grandpa and be uniquely bonded to Isaac in the best and deepest sense of the grandfather/grandson relationship.

Recently Isaac came for a visit. At the airport I waited in a gathering of others to meet loved ones. Suddenly, and at a distance, little Isaac came around the corner and we saw each other. Isaac's face lit up with a huge smile and he came running, arms outstretched, to the one guy in the crowd he uniquely knows as "Grandpa." It was clear that among those many travelers and greeters, we belonged to one another, and I experienced the deepest joy a grandpa can know.

—John C.

Our grandchildren accept us for ourselves, without rebuke or effort to change us,
as no one in our entire lives has ever done, not our parents, siblings,
spouses, friends—and hardly ever our own grown children.
—RUTH GOODE

We Never Outgrow Grandpa's Comfort

My grandfather's overzealous attempt to cook the largest pancakes ever witnessed in a private residence was too much for me and my small, child-sized tummy. After a few attempts to actually clean my plate, I was determined to never eat a pancake again. Now, many years later, breakfast is my favorite meal. When at a restaurant, I occasionally indulge in a pancake platter. And as they bring out a teeny-tiny stack that barely measures the circumference of a saucer let alone a full dinner plate, I have to laugh, "You call *these* pancakes?"

Apparently pancake tales run like amber syrup through the grandfather memories of other people. When I asked a good friend about her grandfather recently, she first thought of a pancake story. As we talked, I realized her story, like mine, was really about the legacy of comfort and care that loving grandpas pass along to their grandchildren whether in the kitchen, out in nature, or on the park bench. When we feel safe with these gentle men, the memories are dear to us.

My friend Dawn recalls being treated to the delight of pancakes no matter what time of day they visited her Grandpa Pete. He was a patient, enduring man whose life was not easy, yet he readily served up kindness with a side of his homemade syrup as the head cook at a small Alaskan airport café. Nontravelers would make the trip to the airport just to eat his fixin's.

One day, as a young adult, Dawn was feeling a bit homesick for the comfort of family. She called Grandpa Pete to get his pancake and syrup recipes. Unable to locate all the ingredients where she lived, Dawn drew consolation she needed from the voice of her grandfather. But her craving for the special pancakes and syrup remained.

Days later, Dawn went to her mailbox and was amazed to find a package from her grandpa. Despite having recently suffered a stroke, he had carefully wrapped each ingredient in newspaper and bundled it all up for Dawn. It was some time later that Dawn found out he had walked several miles to purchase the special flavoring she needed. Only a grandfather's heart could understand the comfort this would bring a grown child many miles away from home.

Grandpa Pete's Syrup

2 cups sugar
1 cup water
dash salt
1 splash lemon juice
Mapleline maple flavoring

Bring water to a boil, add sugar, and stir while sugar dissolves. Add a dash of salt and a splash of lemon juice. Add Mapleline to color and flavor as desired. Remove from heat and serve over your grandpa's pancakes.

What children need most are the essentials that grandparents provide in abundance. They give unconditional love, kindness, patience, humor, comfort, lessons in life. And, most importantly, cookies.

—Rudolph Giuliani

We find in life exactly
what we put into it.
—Ralph Waldo Emerson

My grandfather once told me that there are two
kinds of people: those who work and those who
take the credit. He told me to try to be in the
first group; there was less competition there.
—Indira Gandhi

Make Yourself Useful

My grandpa taught me many lessons at the dinner table. He would sit next to me, hold up his hand, and say, "Remember in all things, be the thumb and not the pinky. The thumb is what distinguishes man from all other animals—it is what allows us to invent and create all that we see in civilization. The pinky, however, wouldn't be terribly missed if it was gone—we would still be able to live our lives without too much interruption."

As a young girl hearing this, I thought that my grandfather was simply teaching me to be number one at whatever I did. But when I grew older and thought about the lesson, I realized Grandpa was illustrating a more significant lesson. He was teaching me to be useful, to serve, and to contribute to my community and to improve the lives of others. He was teaching me to make my life useful for the greater good.

—Jean C.

As soon as they entered the hut and Heidi was released from her wrapping she said, "Grandfather, tomorrow we must take the hammer and plenty of long nails to fix the grandmother's shutters and all the loose boards because her house rattles and shakes all over!"

"Must we, indeed! And who told you so?" inquired the grandfather.

"Nobody told me but I know myself," replied Heidi, "for everything is loose and if the grandmother cannot sleep she is afraid that any minute the house will fall down on their heads. And for her everything is dark and she thinks that nobody can ever make it light for her again; but you can do it, Grandfather, I am sure. Think how sad it is for her always having to sit in the dark, and being frightened; and only you can help her. Tomorrow we will go and help her, won't we, Grandfather?"

Heidi clung tightly to the grandfather and looked up at him with eagerness and confidence. For a little while the old man looked down at the child, then he said, "Yes, Heidi, we will go and see about the repairs. We can do that tomorrow."

—Johanna Spyri
Heidi

You Can *Always* Come Home

Sunday Drive

"I used to deliver feed out here," says Dad and we giggle, his girls. We and the blue-finned Chevy know this ode to gravel. It goes before us, insurance for safe passage on roads that sound friendly, drive ornery.

"Hold your arm out the window," I say to my sister and freckles erupt like solar flares, cooling to permanence in the wind-wake of our Amelia Earhart hands.

Red-Wing Blackbird scoffs but Horse is appreciative. "Wave to the nice pony," I say and Grandpa, provider of Oreos, cold milk, and new kittens, thinks our salutation his as we glide, blue hawk into the shade of his barn.

—DAWN FLORA CADWELL

A man travels the world over in search of what he needs and returns home to find it.
—GEORGE MOORE

"Here we are," said Father.

"Here we are at the farm."

"Oh, oh," said Jane.

"Here we are at the farm.

I see Grandmother.

I see Grandfather."

—WILLIAMS GRAY AND MAY HILL ARBUTHNOT
Fun with Dick and Jane

Mid pleasures and palaces though we may roam,
Be it ever so humble, there's no place like home.
—JOHN HOWARD PAYNE

Where we love is home—home that our feet
may leave, but not our hearts.
—OLIVER WENDELL HOLMES

Memory
My childhood's home I see again,
And sadden with the view;
And still, as memory crowds my brain,
There's pleasure in it, too.
—ABRAHAM LINCOLN

A Boy's Thanksgiving Day
Over the river, and through the wood,
To Grandfather's house we go;
The horse knows the way to carry the sleigh
through the white and drifted snow.
—LYDIA MARIA CHILD

*When grandparents
enter the door,
discipline flies
out the window.*

—OGDEN NASH

*Some have the gift of song and some
possess the gift of silver speech,
Some have the gift of leadership and
some the ways of life can teach.
And fame and wealth reward their
friends; in jewels are their splendors told,
But in good time their favorites grow
very faint and gray and old.
But there are men who laugh at time
and hold the cruel years at bay;
They romp through life forever young
because they have the gift of play.*

—EDGAR A. GUEST

Creation Is *Our* Playground

My grandfather jokingly referred to his fishing cabin as San Clemente—the name of President Nixon's vacation home. *This* vacation home was a tiny, functional shack placed on the banks of the Nehalem River in Oregon. This lean-to with shingles was so narrow my tiny grandmother would stand by the makeshift counter to fix meals or clean fish and have very little elbow room.

Our trips to the cabin were always joyous and satisfying. When we were out in nature with our grandpa, we tasted a side of life that we didn't get in the suburbs—especially as young girls. My sister recalls careening around the bumpy, back roads in the passenger seat of my grandpa's red and white Jeep and not once being afraid. We felt safe in this rustic setting because our grandfather was capable, shrewd, and wise.

Grown men still talk with deep affection of my grandpa's love of nature and his willingness to share the joy of it with others. The times he spent with fishing and hunting buddies—including my very nature-adept grandma—were surely the most sacred times of his vibrant life.

To this day, when I start daydreaming, I imagine lying against a warm boulder near the river, the afternoon sun shining brightly, and my eyes squinting tight while the rest of my body relaxes and soaks up the outdoors. I can hear my grandfather's voice, his laughter. I can nearly taste the smoked salmon. And my heart fills with joy.

I'm going to show you a little trick, he said.
This fruit jar will be our flashlight on the walk back.
It would be easy for their grandfather to make them look foolish
if they asked a foolish question, so they waited, watching
quietly for the secret behind the trick. Whatever it might be.
The first hint was a sudden green glow in the dark grass,
then a brighter, clearer light as the firefly rose.

—Jim Heynen
The One-Room Schoolhouse

A Grandfather's *Advice* for Life

- Learn to be friendly toward others. Be the first to smile and introduce yourself. Remember names of new acquaintances and call them by name.

- On the job, always project happiness and enthusiasm. Make those you work for or with or those you wait on, feel as though you appreciate them.

- Always tell the truth, even when it's hard.

- Never be too proud to say "I'm sorry" when you've messed up.

- Don't be afraid to lead when you're put in a leadership position.

- Always do the right thing, even if it's seemingly to your disadvantage.

- Stay on top of your circumstances, never under them.

- Loving another person doesn't mean you'll always "feel" in love. Real love is a commitment to another person, regardless of feelings.

- Believe in miracles. You are one.

- When you have a list of things to do, do the toughest one first and get it out of the way.

- Maintain high standards.

- Choose happiness over money. The latter can't buy the former.

- When buying ice cream—always buy the good stuff.

- Ration your TV watching.

- Read the book of Proverbs often.

- Go barefoot on the beach regularly.

- Forgive yourself for the mistakes you make in life.

- Reflect often on the good things in your life and in your youth. Memory can be a great restorative.

*Tell loved ones you love them
and then give them a hug.*
—NICK HARRISON

Treat *Others* with Respect

I remember fondly the times I spent with my Grandpa Dick going fishing or heading out on some adventure. Sometimes I would be lucky enough to run errands with him. Usually it was to go see someone about something Grandpa was interested in checking out or buying. Often the item related to his passion for hunting and fishing. Those details are less clear, but what I remember most was how Grandpa Dick would interact with these strangers, treating them with respect, and listening patiently to what they had to say before asking what he wanted to ask. I feel this was a life lesson that I hope has rubbed off on me.

—Randall B.

I love how my father taught me and teaches my kids how to respect others. He has always had friendships with people of all walks of life. He never places value on the person's position, job, status, or income. He sees every person as God's child.

—Cheri B.

Not a tenth of us who are in business are doing as well as we could if we merely followed the principles that were known to our grandfathers.
—William Feather

The greatest gift we can give one another is rapt attention to one another's existence.
—Sue Atchley Ebaugh

Be Yourself

One afternoon Paw Paw picked up his grand-kids Jared and Morgan from school. It was a dark, gloomy day with a sky that warned of showers. The kids settled into the car and pre-pared themselves for whatever adventure Paw Paw would take them on...when all at once it started pouring down rain. Texas rains can take everyone by surprise, but Paw Paw didn't seem fazed at all—in fact, he kept his window down. Since Paw Paw has a different way of doing most things, Jared and Morgan at first thought this ought to be quite interesting. But as a bright and straightforward first grader, Morgan was unable to stand the situation one moment longer. She stated the obvious, "Paw Paw, your window is down!" So their grandfather with his usual quiet demeanor pulled into the nearest gas station, got out of the car, and retrieved the lid from a big plastic tub from the trunk. He then got back in the car and used his elbow to prop the lid up like a window as he drove.

You see, Paw Paw's window was broken, and he had not fixed it yet. Jared thought to himself, *This man is so clever.* And Morgan thought to herself, *This is very different.*

Looking back on this story, Jared and Morgan love to laugh at how nothing ever seems to be any big deal to Paw Paw. He always has a plan. More importantly, Paw Paw is always himself, ready to do things his own creative way. He never worries about what something looks like, what others think, or whether his way is different. And best of all, he encourages all his grandkids—Jared, Morgan, Avery, and Lindy—to never com-promise who they are, what they believe, and how they approach life. Even when it rains.

—Jared and Morgan Lyda

A child needs a grandparent, anybody's grandparent, to grow a little more securely into an unfamiliar world.
—CHARLES AND ANN MORSE

A cheerful heart makes its own blue sky.
—AUTHOR UNKNOWN

You have to do your own growing no
matter how tall your grandfather was.
—ABRAHAM LINCOLN

Children need models more
than they need critics.
—JOSEPH JOUBERT

*Perfection consists not in
doing extraordinary things,
but in doing ordinary things
extraordinarily well.*
—ANTOINE ARNAULD

Whenever I think about my grandfather, I am encouraged; his life has always been a shining example for us grandkids to follow. He grew up as R.H. (Bob) Hawkins in Oklahoma, the youngest of many siblings. His father was already in his fifties by the time he was born, and he took great disinterest in him, never believing that Grandpa could amount to anything.

After serving in the army as a young man, my grandfather married my grandmother, Shirley, and began a successful career in Christian book publishing. He has worked with many influential people and has always kept a focus on the heart and needs of the book readers. His vision led him to start his own company, Harvest House Publishers, which sells books offering comfort, encouragement, and inspiration throughout the world.

This man who did not have love and respect in his childhood family now has three children and four grandchildren, all of whom love and admire him very much for who he is and who he has become. My grandfather's legacy has been a truly astounding one—he not only amounted to something, but his success far surpassed anything either of his parents could ever have expected. His servant-leadership and perseverance is an inspiration in my life and in the lives of many people.

—Ben Hawkins

Let your grandchildren know, through work and deeds, that the bond of affection which attaches the two of you to one another can never be broken.

—ARTHUR KORNHABER

Sharing Makes Life Better

As a child, I spent many Fourth of July weekends with my mother's side of the family. Cousins, aunts, and uncles came to my grandpa's cabin in Merrilan, Wisconsin. My grandfather bought the small and in-need-of-repair house because he had a vision—he wanted to share this wonderful place with the family he loved so much.

When Grandpa retired from teaching mathematics and physics, he worked hard on the cabin, adding rooms and areas for the summer visitors. Over time, he also acquired a collection of used sports equipment for us. However, there was a rule—to make it fair, you had to share. Sharing with 50 relatives wasn't easy—but we did it.

That is…until the year of the Green Tandem.

A 1950 single-speed Schwinn to be exact. This two-seater was the coolest thing I'd ever seen. It was jet green with white-striped, black, fat tires and handlebars with streamers. And *everyone* wanted to ride it.

The desire to share soon conflicted with the novelty of the GT—the older cousins were hogging it. As we stood around arguing about who got to ride next, Grandpa arrived on the scene. At first, he didn't say a word. Then he took the bike, put it in the garage, and said, "We are not going to use the bike today."

Everyone was unhappy, me especially—I was next to use it! But after I gave the situation some thought, I was glad he stepped in; I knew he would take care of what needed to be done.

The next morning after breakfast I rushed down to the garage and was relieved to find the GT standing ready for use. Above it was a sign-up sheet on a clipboard, two sharpened pencils, and instructions: Fill in the names of who will use the bike and designate which half hour. It was a simple solution that everyone honored.

My grandfather's fair approach to the Green Tandem dilemma allowed us an opportunity to make things right. It was his way of being a lifelong teacher. His lesson that summer helped us get the most out of the experience and out of our time together.

—Morgan C.

My grandfather always taught us that the first step of wisdom is silence, and the second step is listening.
—ARNOLD BETTERMAN

Never hold back the urge to share a story from your past. And do not ever resist the desire to pick up the phone and call your grandchild. Each is an offering of a memory and is truly priceless.
—BOB AND EMILIE BARNES

LEMONADE
~~25¢~~ 10¢

It is the malady of our age that the young are so busy teaching us that they have no time left to learn.
—Eric Hoffer

An aim in life is the only fortune worth the finding; and it is not to be found in foreign lands, but in the heart itself.
—Robert Louis Stevenson

It Is Never Too Late To Learn New Things

Dapper in his small sport coat and fedora hat, Granddad drew respected glances as he walked briskly from the pharmacy coffee shop to his two-man insurance office straight up Main. An unassuming businessman in a small Oregon town, he passed a narrow storefront that used to house the children's clothing shop he and my grandmother ran, the corner variety store his daughter still operated, and the large, charred lot that once held the J.C. Penney store he managed. It had been a productive life.

At age 70, Granddad was about to retire. Friends and family quizzed the slight, white-haired, balding man about how he would spend this chapter of his life. Would he make custom buttons and belts in the spare room as he had in the past? Or take in bookkeeping work? Or maybe he would have more time to hold my three sisters and me by our armpits and swing us way up high and down low between his legs and then up again until we giggled with delight.

But Granddad surprised us all by announcing that he would draw. We had watched this former class valedictorian make calculations in business ledgers, build household stools and bookcases, and upholster small chairs, but we had never seen him draw. Undaunted, Granddad purchased a handful of art pencils and began meticulously sketching the weathered faces of Native Americans, Eskimos, and others who graced the pages of travel magazines such as *National Geographic.* Soon he was selling charcoal and colored pencil sketches of people, animals, and landscapes at local art fairs. His hand-drawn note cards and framed works became popular.

Though he has been gone for more than 20 years, Granddad's legacy lives on in the beauty of the sketches that hang in area homes and offices, and in the lives of his grandchildren—he inspired all of us to mine the gifts and talents we are given and to never stop learning.

—Nancy S.

Learning softeneth the heart and breedeth gentleness and charity.

—MARK TWAIN
The Prince and the Pauper

Live Graciously

My grandfather was always sweet to his grand-kids. He teased us. He listened to us. He appreciated our silly gifts like the baseball cap with the fabric fish sticking through it. But I think we always recognized what a strong man he was and had been in his early years—strong in physical strength and in spirit.

Mom tells us how Grandpa, a young boxer, used to do push-ups with her sitting on his back. She always trusted him to hold her up. And if Grandpa, a former union organizer, asked my mom or her older sister Carol to do something, they knew to do it and do it well. I doubt there was much back talk heard in that home.

But as my grandfather grew older, the tough-ness gave way to pure graciousness. When this avid hunter and fisherman no longer had the vision to pursue his outdoor passions, he settled for opportunities to go on recreational trips with his younger friends as an observer, a mentor. When a tragic fire burned much of his home, he accepted help and advice and temporary shelter.

My mom says she always felt like the "kid" around my grandpa. After so many years as an adult, this was the emotional role she took on when in her strong father's presence. But as Grandpa had to endure the losses and changes that age bestows, he gave her the greatest gift a father could pass along—respect. Even when she faced decisions on his behalf that seemed overwhelming, she received his complete faith. His grace allowed a grown kid to feel loved and needed.

There once was a man who did push-ups with a little girl on his back.

And the day came when he trusted her to hold him up.

You cannot purchase happiness,
It's something you must earn;
Give happiness to other folks,
And get joy in return.
—Harold G. Hopper

Duty makes us do things well,
but love makes us do them beautifully.
—Phillips Brooks

You will find as you look back upon life that the moments when you have really
lived are the moments when you have done things in the spirit of love.
—Henry Drummond

One of the most powerful handclasps
is that of a new grandbaby around
the finger of a grandfather.
—JOY HARGROVE

Giving is the secret of a healthy life...
not necessarily money, but encouragement,
sympathy, and understanding.
—JOHN D. ROCKEFELLER

Give a little love to a child,
and you get a great deal back.
—JOHN RUSKIN

No cowboy was ever faster
on the draw than a grandparent
pulling a baby picture out of a wallet.
—AUTHOR UNKNOWN

What a wonderful contribution our grandmothers
and grandfathers can make if they will share some
of the rich experiences and their testimonies with
their children and grandchildren.
—VAUGHN J. FEATHERSTONE